I Can Draw...
Cars & Trucks

Artwork by Terry Longhurst

Text by Amanda O'Neill

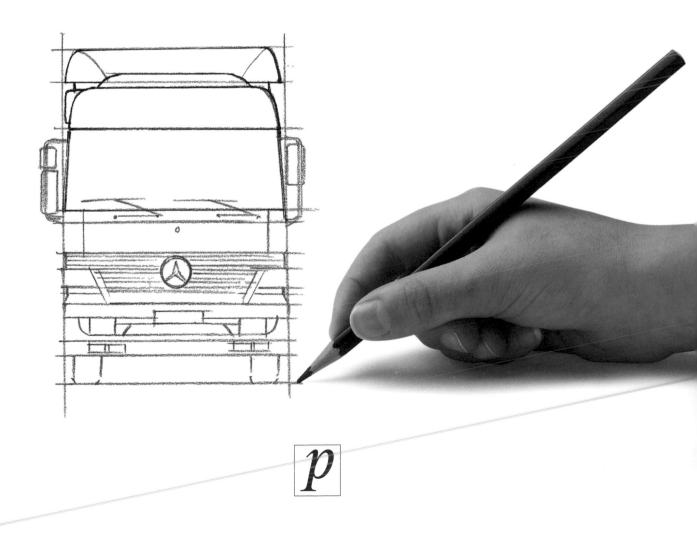

p

This is a Parragon Publishing Book
This edition published in 2004

Parragon Publishing
Queen Street House
4 Queen Street
Bath BA1 1HE, UK

Copyright © Parragon 2001

Designed, packaged, and produced by
Touchstone

ISBN 0-75257-282-2

Artwork by Terry Longhurst
Text by Amanda O'Neill
Edited by Philip de Ste. Croix

Printed in China

About this book

Everybody can enjoy drawing, but sometimes it's hard to know where to begin. The subject you want to draw can look very complicated. This book shows you how to start, by breaking down your subject into a series of simple shapes.

The tools you need are very simple. The basic requirements are paper and pencils. Very thin paper wears through if you have to rub out a line, so choose paper that is thick enough to work on. Pencils come with different leads, from very hard to very soft. Very hard pencils give a clean, thin line which is best for finishing drawings. Very soft ones give a thicker, darker line. You will probably find a medium pencil most useful.

If you want to color in your drawing, you have the choice of paints, colored inks, or felt-tip pens. Fine felt-tips are useful for drawing outlines, thick felt-tips are better for coloring in.

The most important tool you have is your own eyes. The mistake many people make is to draw what they think something looks like, instead of really looking at it carefully first. Half the secret of making your drawing look good is getting the proportions right. Study your subject before you start, and break it down in your mind into sections. Check how much bigger, or longer, or shorter, one part is than another. Notice where one part joins another, and at what angle. See where there are flowing curves, and where there are straight lines.

The step-by-step drawings in this book show you exactly how to do this. Each subject is broken down into easy stages, so you can build up your drawing one piece at a time. Look carefully at each shape before – and after – you draw it. If you find you have drawn it the wrong size or in the wrong place, correct it before you go on. Then the next shape will fit into place, and piece-by-piece you can build up a fantastic picture.

Ferrari F50

Be careful to get these first shapes right.

Supercars like this are more like racers than ordinary passenger vehicles. This F50 is built with the same care as Ferrari's famous racing cars, with sleek, aggressive lines and a powerful engine.

Start to build up the front of the car. The powerful hood takes up much of the drawing.

Draw in arched shapes for the wheels.

This is a long, low car, so be careful not to make the roof too high.

Now add the spoiler on the back of the car.

Smooth, flowing curves reduce air resistance and increase speed.

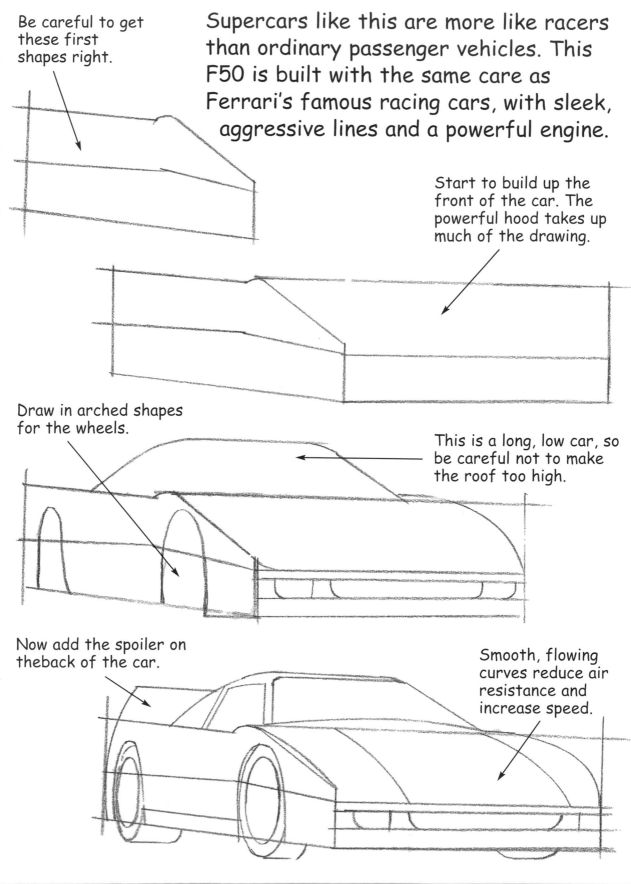

The headlamps are flush with the hood, so they do not break up its smooth lines.

This scoop directs air to cool the massive rear-mounted V12 engine.

The sloping windshield has a single huge wiper.

Now you can ink in your outlines.

The engine is housed behind the driver, above the rear wheels. This makes the car perfectly balanced.

Speed limits on the roads mean few drivers will get the chance to try out this supercar's top speed of 200mph.

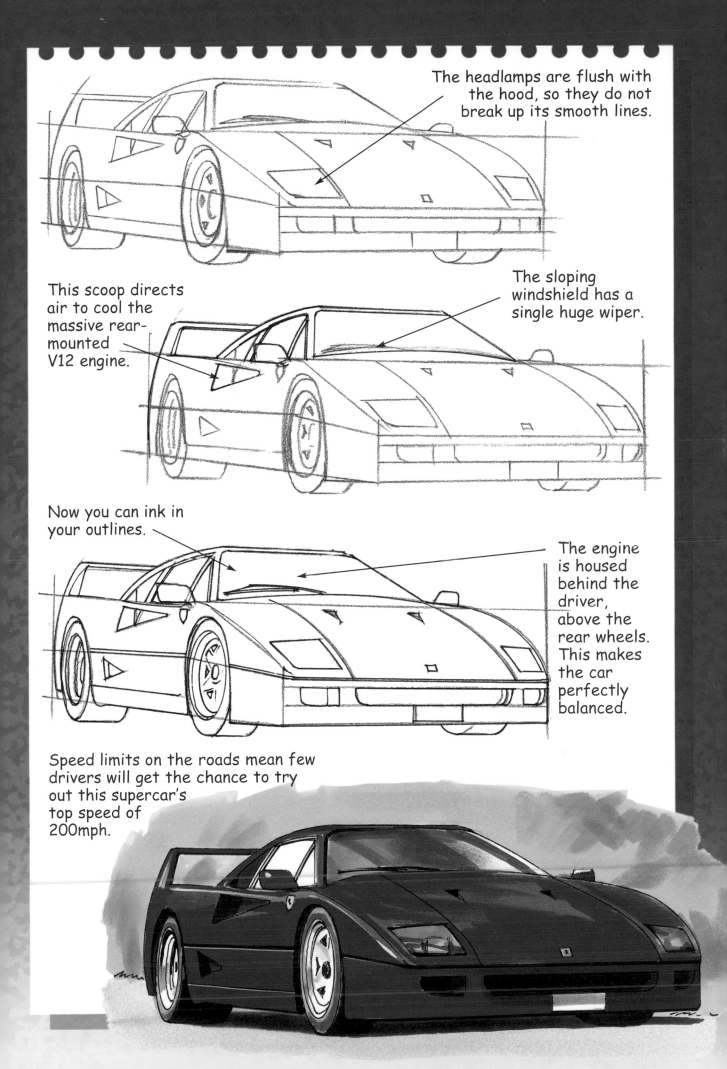

Excavator

A familiar vehicle on construction sites, the earthmover clears the ground of rubble and moves vast quantities of soil to enable foundation work to begin. A skilled operator sits in the central cab which pivots full circle on the sturdy 'caterpillar' tracks.

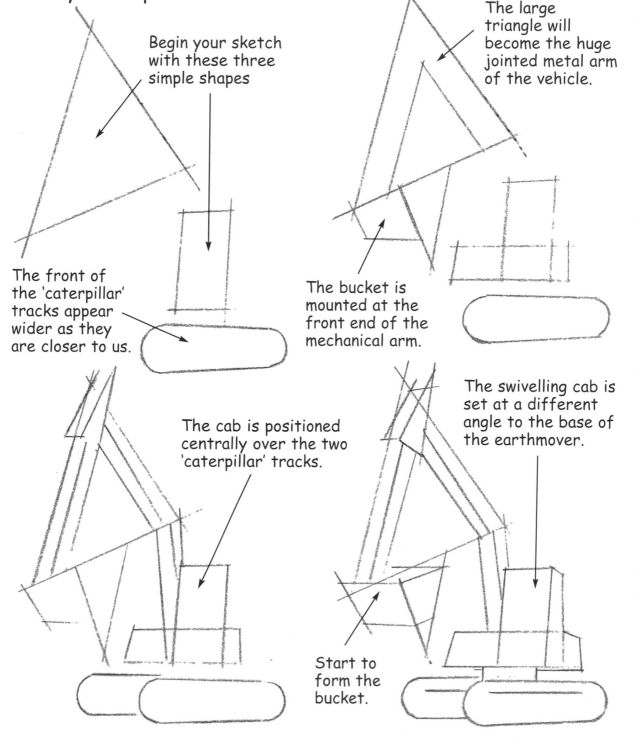

Begin your sketch with these three simple shapes

The large triangle will become the huge jointed metal arm of the vehicle.

The front of the 'caterpillar' tracks appear wider as they are closer to us.

The bucket is mounted at the front end of the mechanical arm.

The cab is positioned centrally over the two 'caterpillar' tracks.

The swivelling cab is set at a different angle to the base of the earthmover.

Start to form the bucket.

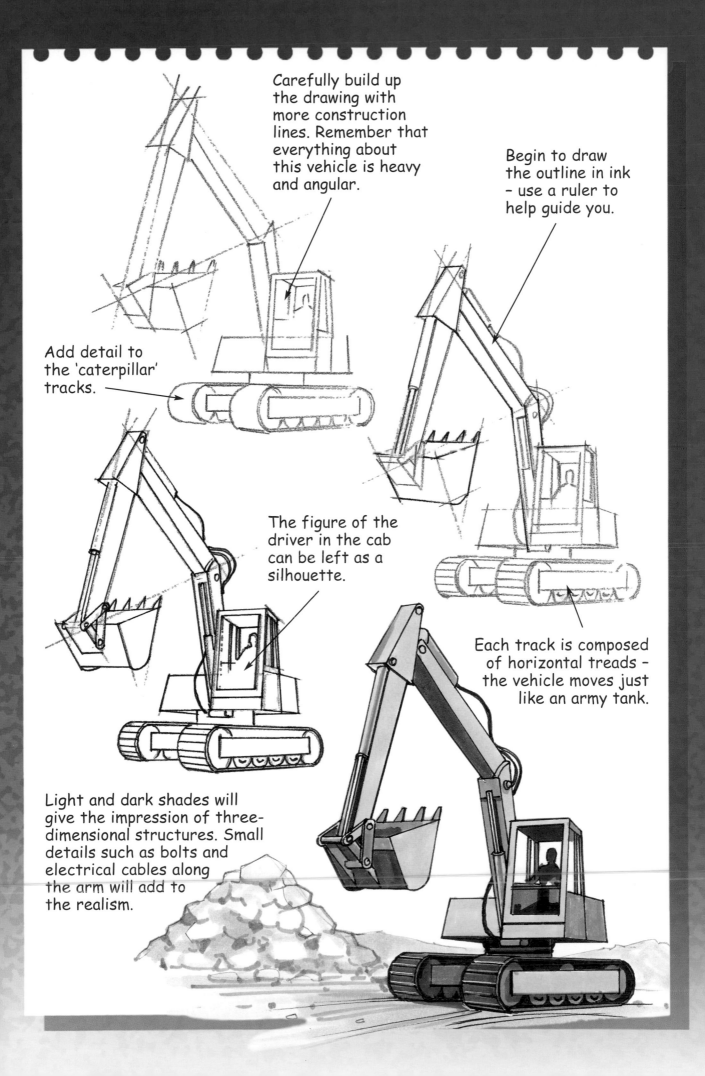

Carefully build up the drawing with more construction lines. Remember that everything about this vehicle is heavy and angular.

Begin to draw the outline in ink – use a ruler to help guide you.

Add detail to the 'caterpillar' tracks.

The figure of the driver in the cab can be left as a silhouette.

Each track is composed of horizontal treads – the vehicle moves just like an army tank.

Light and dark shades will give the impression of three-dimensional structures. Small details such as bolts and electrical cables along the arm will add to the realism.

Mini Cooper

Introduced in 1961, this is the rally version of the famous Mini. Rally cars, designed for racing on public roads, may look very similar to standard models – but they are much faster, with more powerful engines.

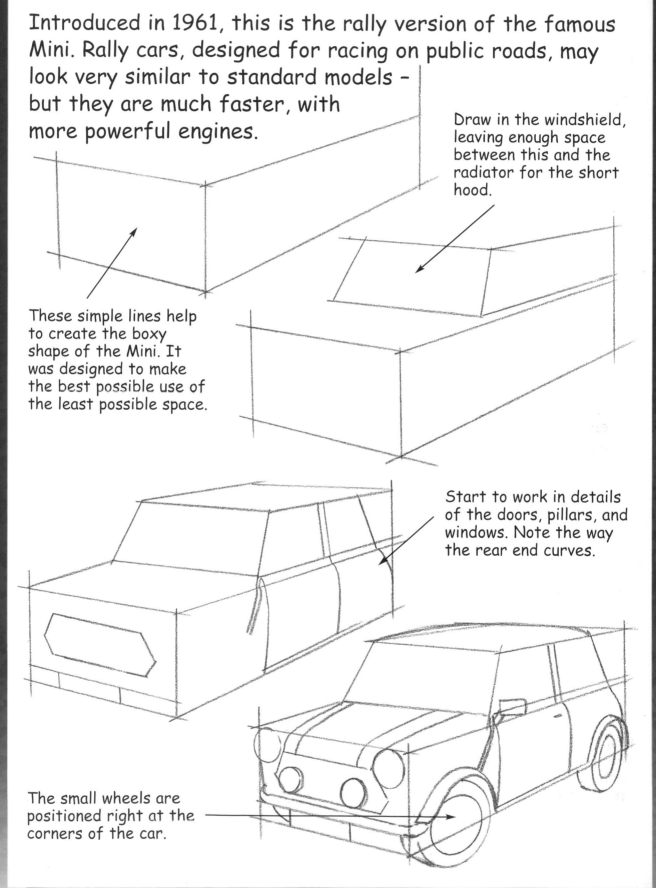

Draw in the windshield, leaving enough space between this and the radiator for the short hood.

These simple lines help to create the boxy shape of the Mini. It was designed to make the best possible use of the least possible space.

Start to work in details of the doors, pillars, and windows. Note the way the rear end curves.

The small wheels are positioned right at the corners of the car.

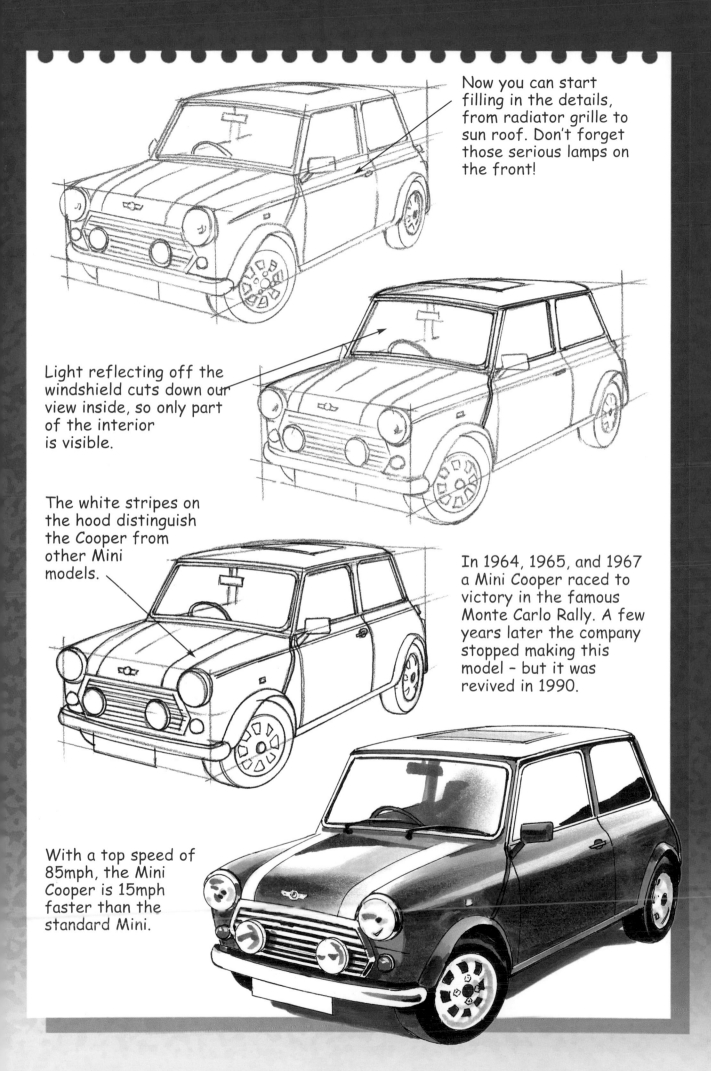

Now you can start filling in the details, from radiator grille to sun roof. Don't forget those serious lamps on the front!

Light reflecting off the windshield cuts down our view inside, so only part of the interior is visible.

The white stripes on the hood distinguish the Cooper from other Mini models.

In 1964, 1965, and 1967 a Mini Cooper raced to victory in the famous Monte Carlo Rally. A few years later the company stopped making this model – but it was revived in 1990.

With a top speed of 85mph, the Mini Cooper is 15mph faster than the standard Mini.

Mercedes-Benz Truck

Trucks carry nearly all the goods and materials we use. They are big, heavy vehicles, but modern trucks like this are still as streamlined as possible.

At the top is the air deflector. It directs the airstream over the vehicle, so improving the aerodynamics of the truck.

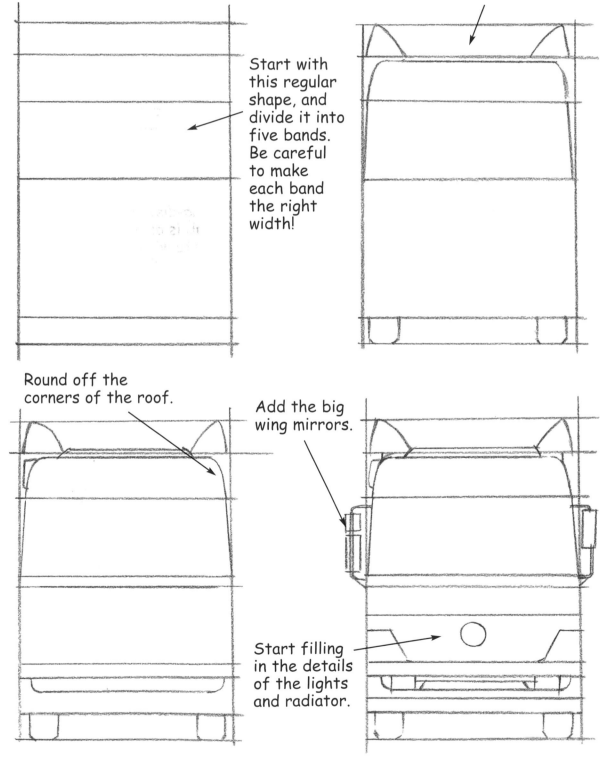

Start with this regular shape, and divide it into five bands. Be careful to make each band the right width!

Round off the corners of the roof.

Add the big wing mirrors.

Start filling in the details of the lights and radiator.

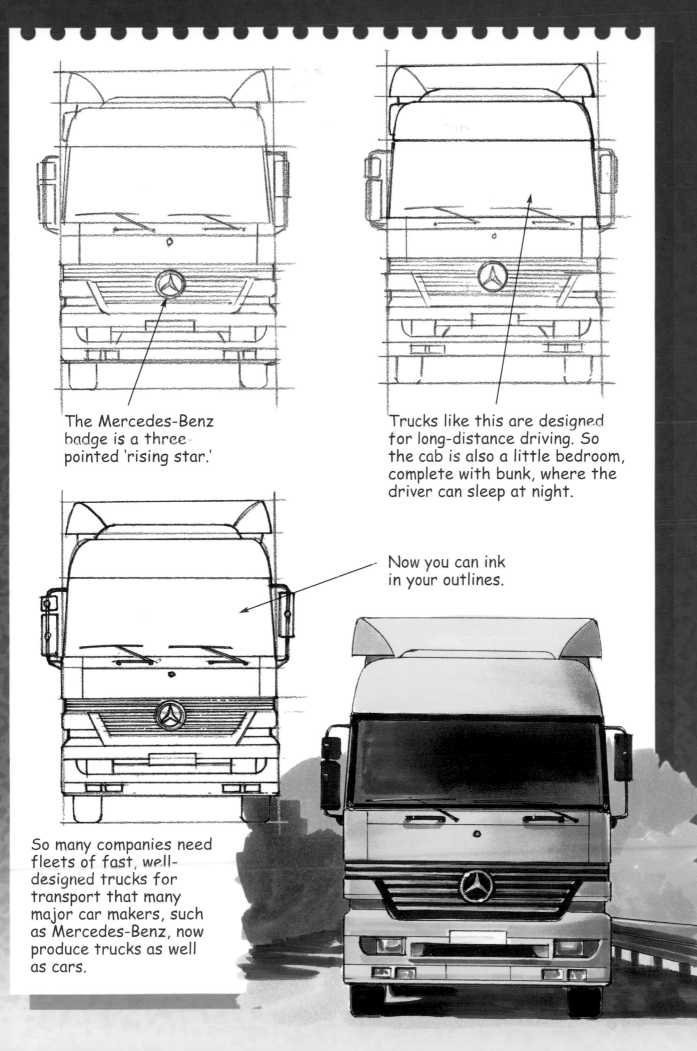

The Mercedes-Benz badge is a three-pointed 'rising star.'

Trucks like this are designed for long-distance driving. So the cab is also a little bedroom, complete with bunk, where the driver can sleep at night.

Now you can ink in your outlines.

So many companies need fleets of fast, well-designed trucks for transport that many major car makers, such as Mercedes-Benz, now produce trucks as well as cars.

Cadillac Coupe de Ville

Big luxury cars like this were very popular in the 1950s. Made for maximum comfort in long-distance travel along America's highways, they looked wonderful, but used incredible amounts of fuel. When gas became more expensive, they went out of fashion.

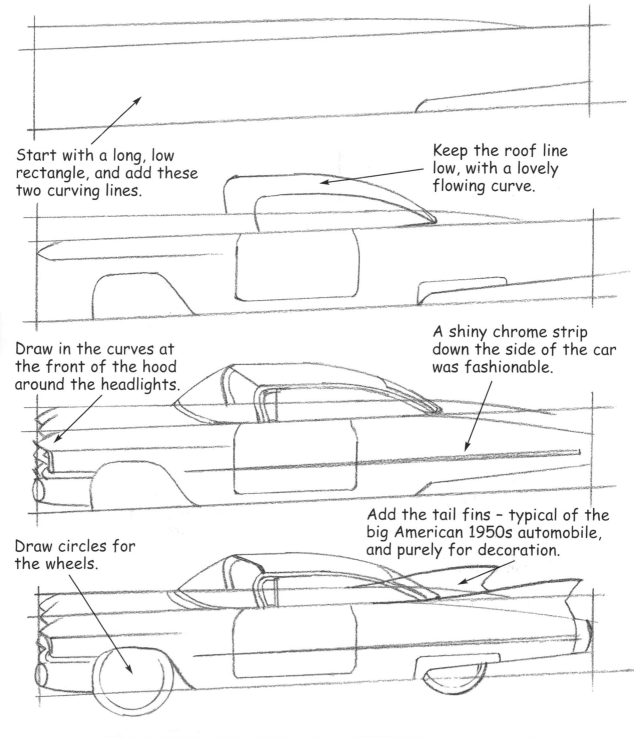

Start with a long, low rectangle, and add these two curving lines.

Keep the roof line low, with a lovely flowing curve.

Draw in the curves at the front of the hood around the headlights.

A shiny chrome strip down the side of the car was fashionable.

Add the tail fins – typical of the big American 1950s automobile, and purely for decoration.

Draw circles for the wheels.

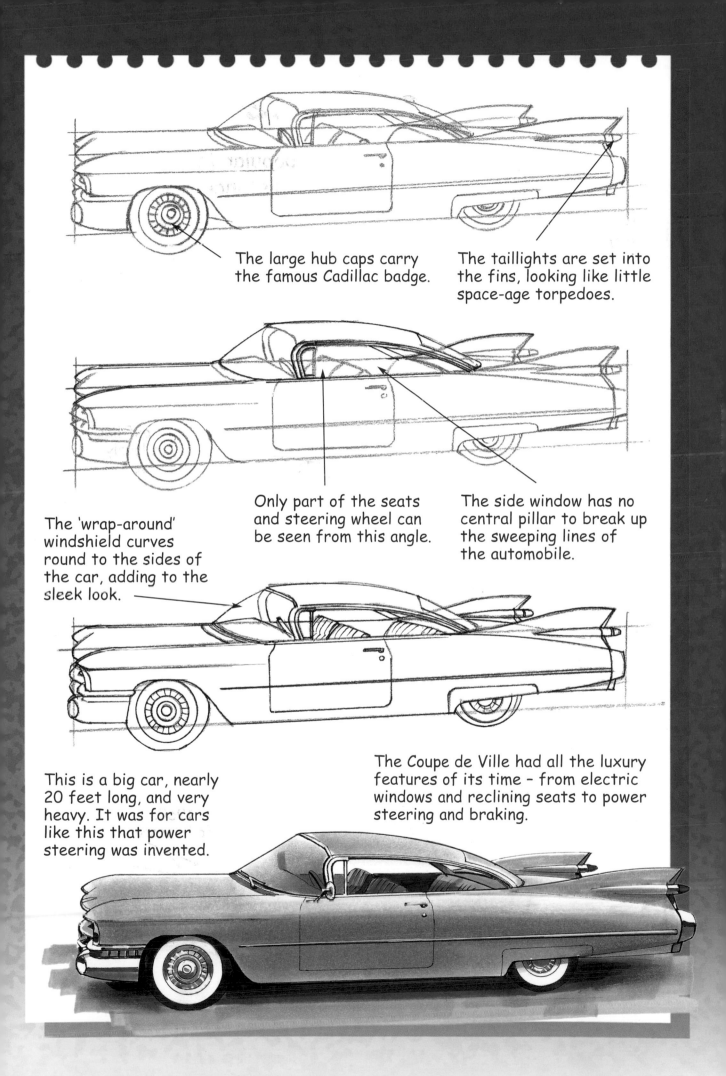

The large hub caps carry the famous Cadillac badge.

The taillights are set into the fins, looking like little space-age torpedoes.

Only part of the seats and steering wheel can be seen from this angle.

The side window has no central pillar to break up the sweeping lines of the automobile.

The 'wrap-around' windshield curves round to the sides of the car, adding to the sleek look.

This is a big car, nearly 20 feet long, and very heavy. It was for cars like this that power steering was invented.

The Coupe de Ville had all the luxury features of its time – from electric windows and reclining seats to power steering and braking.

Transporter

This type of truck consists of two parts. The front part is a 'tractor unit' containing the engine and driver's cab. The back part is a flatbed trailer to carry the load. They are attached by an articulated joint. Different types of load can be fitted on to the flat base of the trailer.

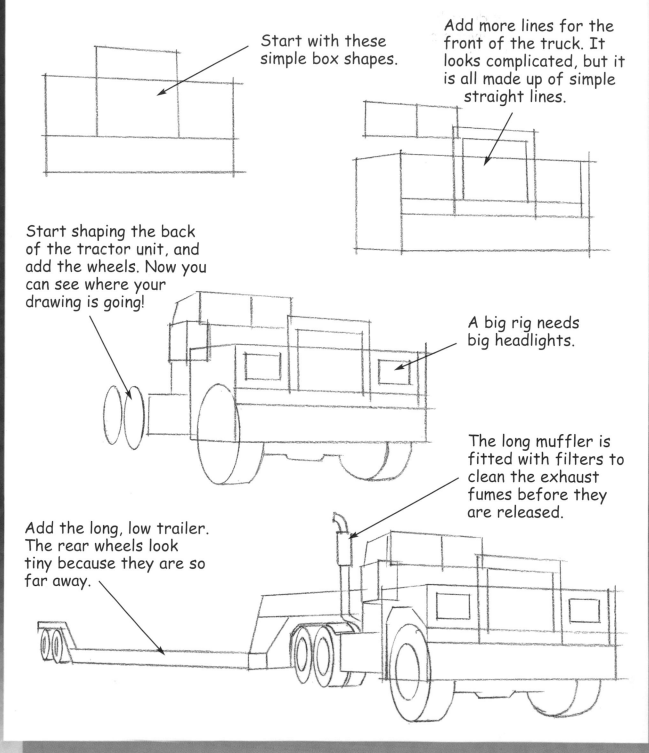

Start with these simple box shapes.

Add more lines for the front of the truck. It looks complicated, but it is all made up of simple straight lines.

Start shaping the back of the tractor unit, and add the wheels. Now you can see where your drawing is going!

A big rig needs big headlights.

The long muffler is fitted with filters to clean the exhaust fumes before they are released.

Add the long, low trailer. The rear wheels look tiny because they are so far away.

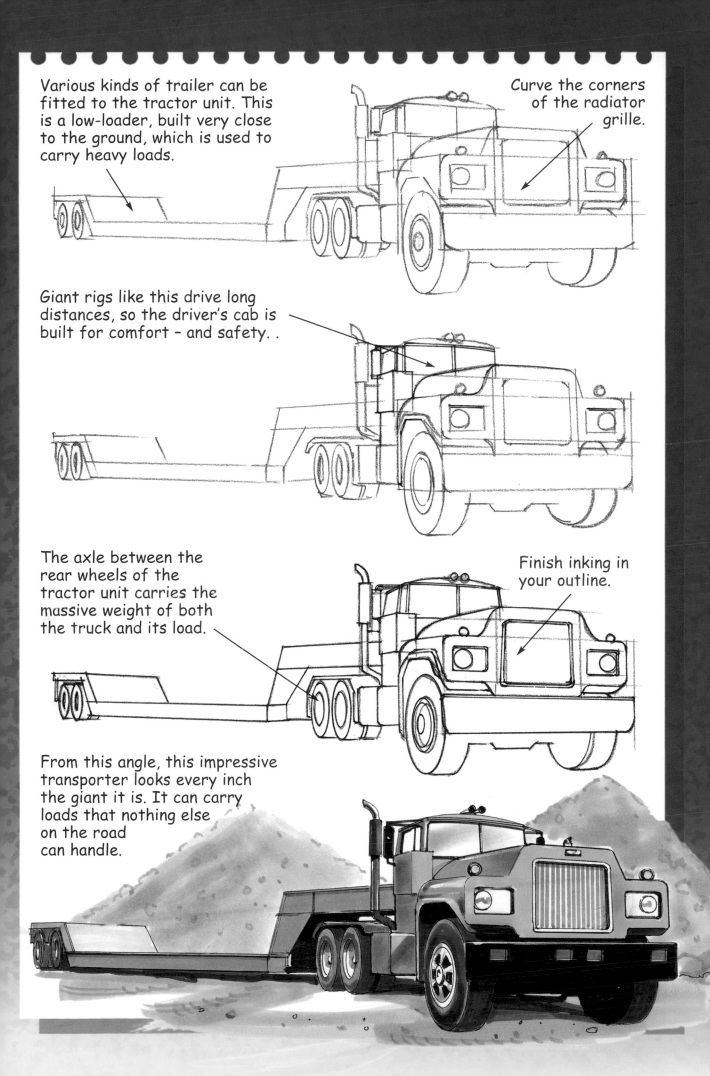

Various kinds of trailer can be fitted to the tractor unit. This is a low-loader, built very close to the ground, which is used to carry heavy loads.

Curve the corners of the radiator grille.

Giant rigs like this drive long distances, so the driver's cab is built for comfort – and safety. .

The axle between the rear wheels of the tractor unit carries the massive weight of both the truck and its load.

Finish inking in your outline.

From this angle, this impressive transporter looks every inch the giant it is. It can carry loads that nothing else on the road can handle.

Waste Disposal Truck

This truck collects garbage from homes and takes it to a disposal site to be burned, dumped, or recycled. The garbage is loaded into a hopper at the back, where it is mechanically crushed. Squashed to a quarter of its original size, it is stored in the main body of the truck.

This square is the driver's cab. Divide it in half with a slanted line.

Start with these three box shapes.

Draw in the large windows and cab door.

Divide up the rear box with these four lines to start making the shape of the hopper.

When garbage is tipped in here, the crusher is operated by a control panel on the outside.

The large cab is designed to hold the driver and a crew of three men. They have enough space to change into their working gear inside the cab.

Draw circles for the wheels.

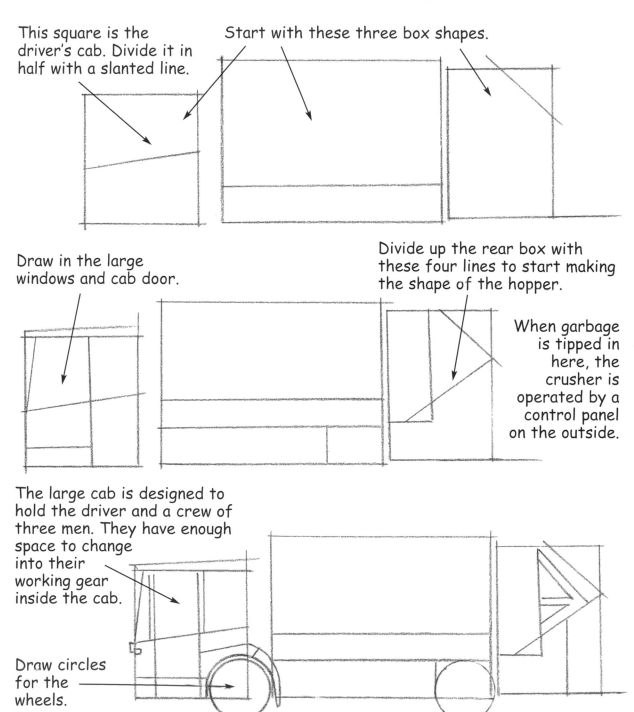

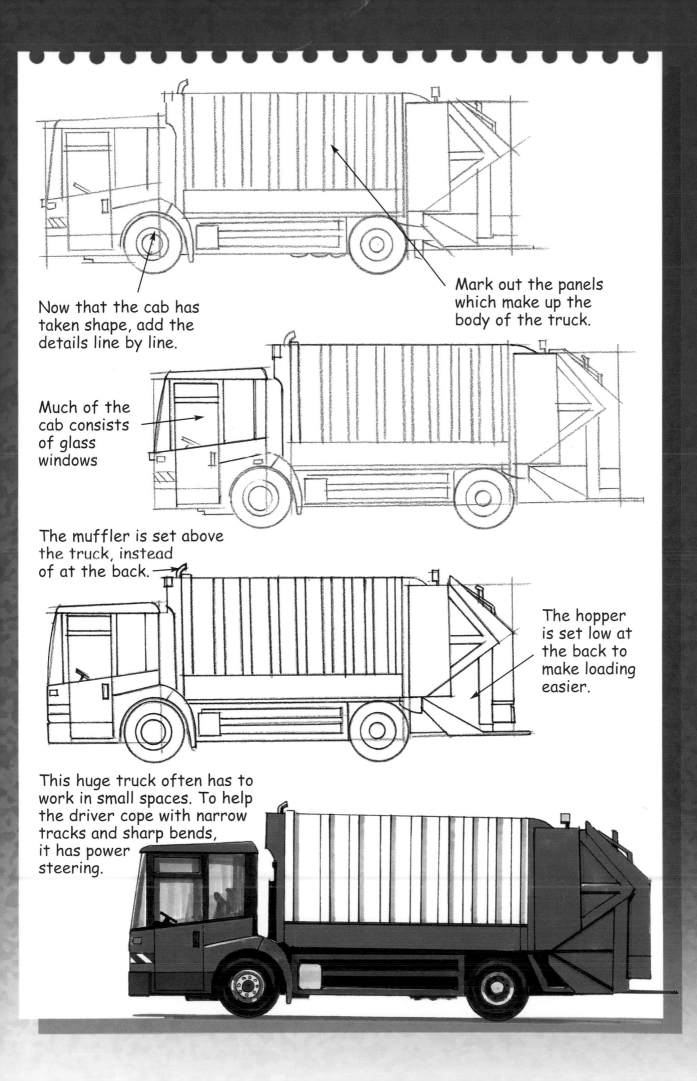

Now that the cab has taken shape, add the details line by line.

Mark out the panels which make up the body of the truck.

Much of the cab consists of glass windows

The muffler is set above the truck, instead of at the back.

The hopper is set low at the back to make loading easier.

This huge truck often has to work in small spaces. To help the driver cope with narrow tracks and sharp bends, it has power steering.

Digger

Tractors can be fitted out with all kinds of machinery for different jobs. They may carry a broad shovel-like blade, for a bulldozer, or a scoop, like this digger. The digger is used to excavate and clear piles of earth and rubble. You will see it on building sites and at road works.

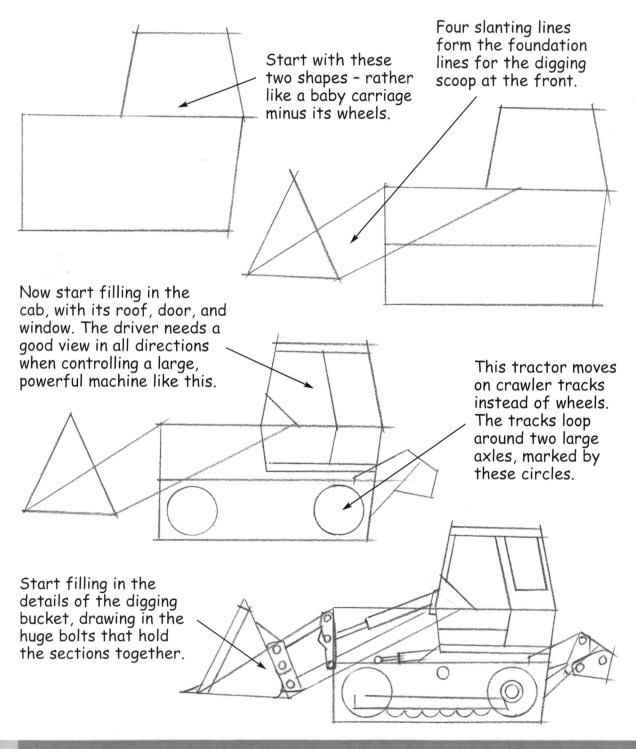

Start with these two shapes – rather like a baby carriage minus its wheels.

Four slanting lines form the foundation lines for the digging scoop at the front.

Now start filling in the cab, with its roof, door, and window. The driver needs a good view in all directions when controlling a large, powerful machine like this.

This tractor moves on crawler tracks instead of wheels. The tracks loop around two large axles, marked by these circles.

Start filling in the details of the digging bucket, drawing in the huge bolts that hold the sections together.

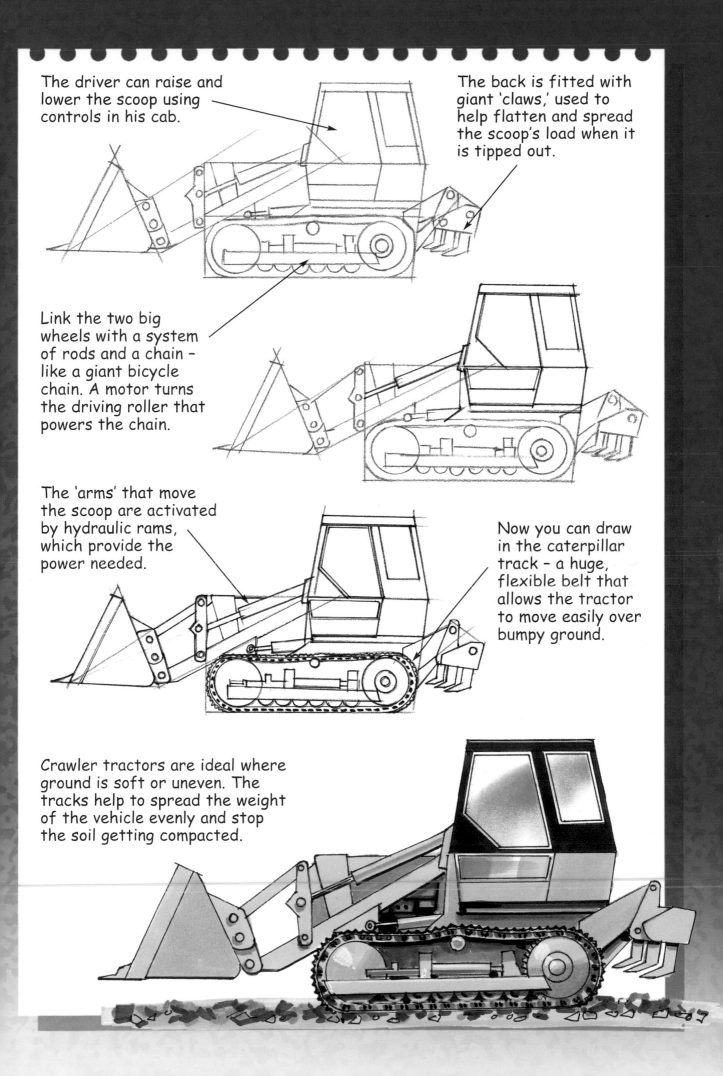

The driver can raise and lower the scoop using controls in his cab.

The back is fitted with giant 'claws,' used to help flatten and spread the scoop's load when it is tipped out.

Link the two big wheels with a system of rods and a chain – like a giant bicycle chain. A motor turns the driving roller that powers the chain.

The 'arms' that move the scoop are activated by hydraulic rams, which provide the power needed.

Now you can draw in the caterpillar track – a huge, flexible belt that allows the tractor to move easily over bumpy ground.

Crawler tractors are ideal where ground is soft or uneven. The tracks help to spread the weight of the vehicle evenly and stop the soil getting compacted.

Land Rover Defender

The Land Rover first appeared in 1948 as a tough 'work-horse' based on the army jeep. Made for rough ground, heavy loads and needing little maintenance, it proved ideal for farmers and the military. Later models include luxury versions like the Discovery and Range Rover.

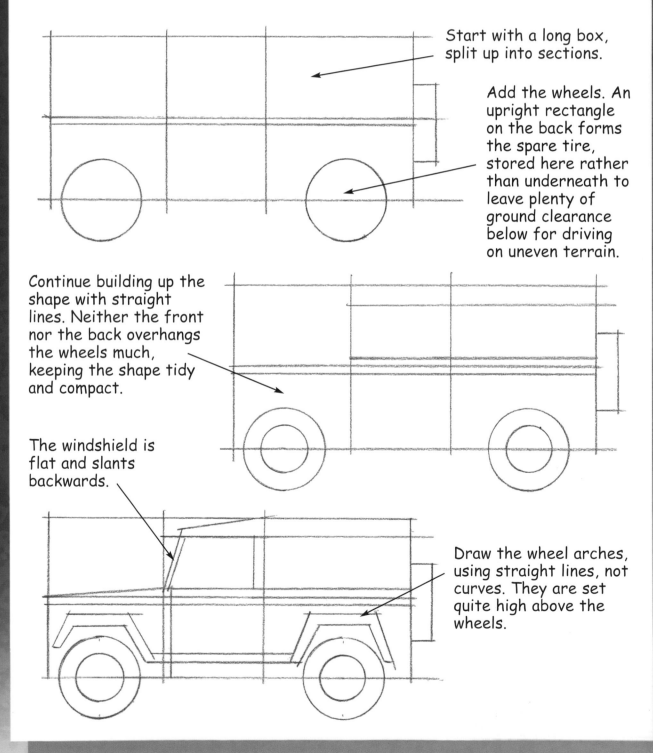

Start with a long box, split up into sections.

Add the wheels. An upright rectangle on the back forms the spare tire, stored here rather than underneath to leave plenty of ground clearance below for driving on uneven terrain.

Continue building up the shape with straight lines. Neither the front nor the back overhangs the wheels much, keeping the shape tidy and compact.

The windshield is flat and slants backwards.

Draw the wheel arches, using straight lines, not curves. They are set quite high above the wheels.

The outline is complete, so now fill in the details. You may see some variation in Defenders on the road: they come with five different body types and three wheelbases, designed for different needs.

Early Land Rovers were all light green – to use up a bulk buy of surplus green paint from the Royal Air Force!

The no-nonsense straight lines of the design are matched in practicality by rust-proof bodywork.

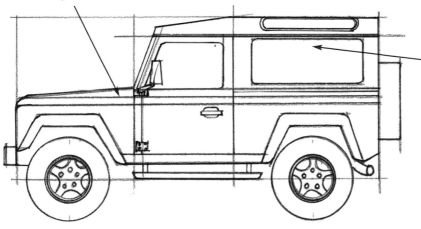

This model has a solid roof, but soft-top versions are available, with a canvas top which can be unfastened to allow bulky loads to be fitted in easily.

The Defender is a lot more than just a farm truck. It has proved ideal for exploration, off-road events and rallies, and military use.

Forklift Truck

This is a handy little work-horse used to transport heavy loads short distances on site. It can carry bricks on a building site, or move pallets from a delivery lorry into a warehouse. It is small enough to carry its load into a building and deliver it directly to the storage bays.

These three simple shapes form the main part of this little vehicle.

The engine is positioned at the rear, so the body sticks out behind.

This upright piece stops the load tipping backward on to the driver.

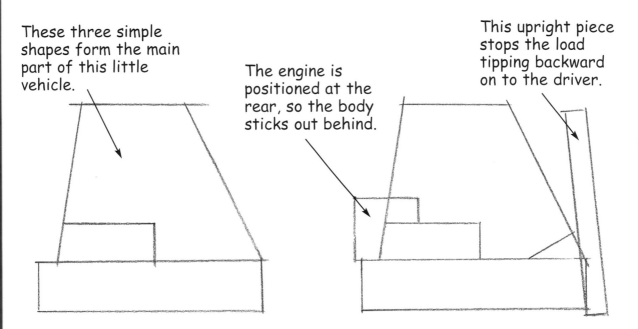

Draw in a simple seat and start on the driver. An oblong and a circle don't look much like a human being – yet. But soon they will!

This long tube is the muffler, placed here to direct fumes away from the driver.

Add arms and legs, curve the shoulders, and suddenly we have quite a convincing driver. The shape in front of him houses the steering column, with the steering wheel under his hands.

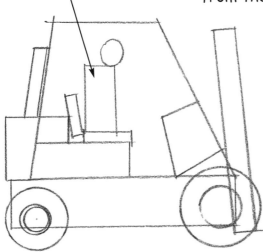

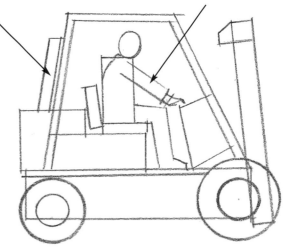

Now add the important bit: the lifting arms. They are quite thin so that the driver can slide them underneath a load. But they are also strong enough to support heavy weights.

Now you can start inking in your final lines. The shapes are very regular so make sure your angles are right.

The driver's seat fits neatly on top of the engine casing. This is a very basic vehicle, covering only short distances, so it does not need a luxury interior.

Finish inking in your outlines. Because the sides are open, to give the driver a good all-round view, you can see right inside the cab and draw more detail inside than you can for other vehicles.

The base is low to the ground, to cut down any risk of the truck tipping over. Since it is not used on rough ground, it does not need high ground clearance.

If big trucks are the work-horses of industry, this is the donkey – small, but strong and very useful. Factories and warehouses depend on it to move heavy loads about.

Tractor

The tractor's shape is simple – two box shapes plus wheels.

Tractors were invented in the late 19th century to do the work of farm-horses, pulling plows and other farm machinery.

Shape the hood with a curving line. It slopes downward so that it does not block the driver's view.

Now add a slant to the front and back of the cab. Early tractors had no cab, just an open seat at the back where the driver was exposed to all weathers.

The back wheels are big, to get a good grip on muddy ground. Draw in the curved fender that protects the back of the cab from mud splashes.

The front wheels are smaller, to make steering easier. Some tractors have caterpillar tracks instead of wheels, to cope with extra rough ground.

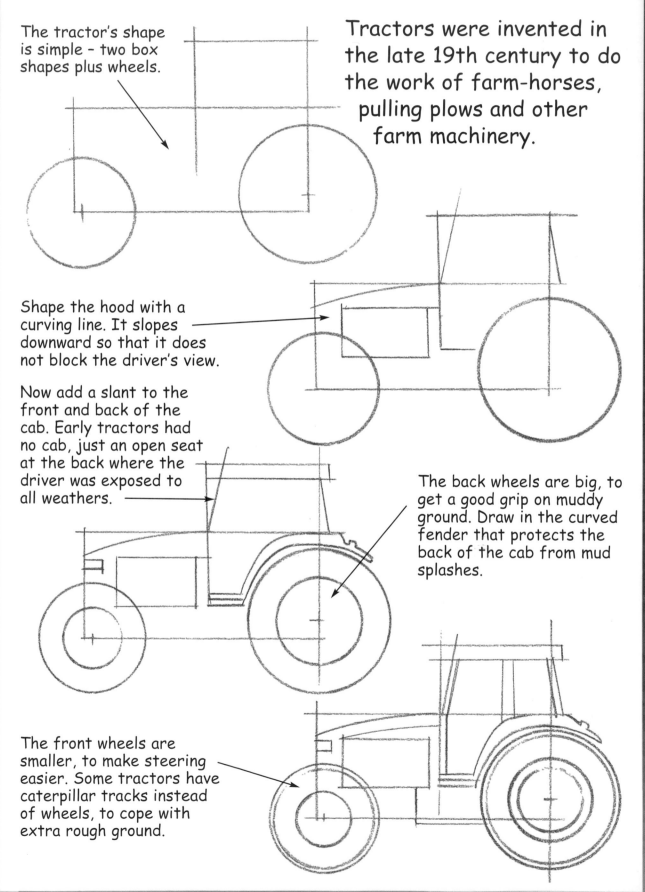

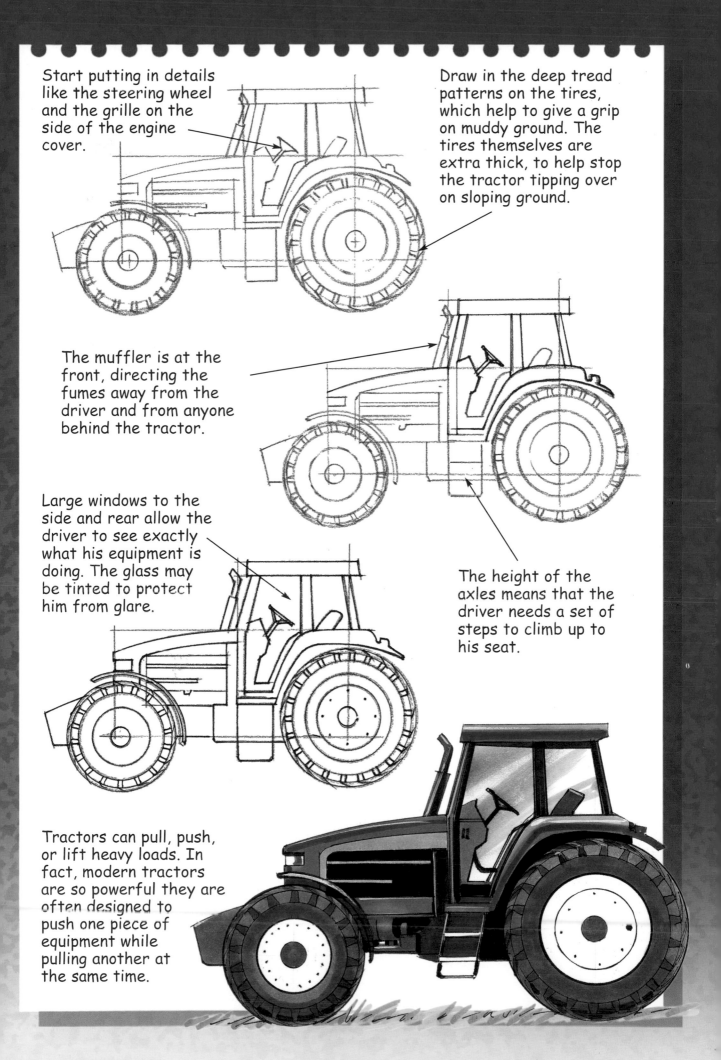

Start putting in details like the steering wheel and the grille on the side of the engine cover.

Draw in the deep tread patterns on the tires, which help to give a grip on muddy ground. The tires themselves are extra thick, to help stop the tractor tipping over on sloping ground.

The muffler is at the front, directing the fumes away from the driver and from anyone behind the tractor.

Large windows to the side and rear allow the driver to see exactly what his equipment is doing. The glass may be tinted to protect him from glare.

The height of the axles means that the driver needs a set of steps to climb up to his seat.

Tractors can pull, push, or lift heavy loads. In fact, modern tractors are so powerful they are often designed to push one piece of equipment while pulling another at the same time.

Jaguar XJS

Most cars are designed in a practical way, for reliability, space, comfort, and fuel economy. Sports cars like this Jaguar are designed for enjoyment. They put speed, power, and good looks first. The XJS first appeared in 1975. It had a big V12 engine and could reach 150mph.

Start with a long box. Divide it into three uneven layers, then mark out the lines of the windows and the position of the wheel arches.

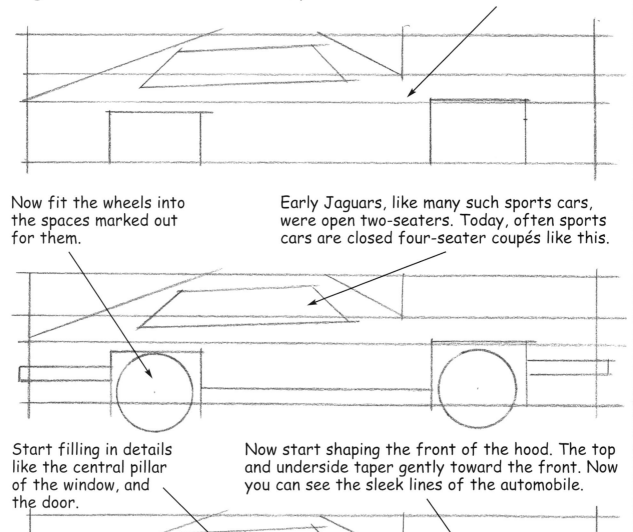

Now fit the wheels into the spaces marked out for them.

Early Jaguars, like many such sports cars, were open two-seaters. Today, often sports cars are closed four-seater coupés like this.

Start filling in details like the central pillar of the window, and the door.

Now start shaping the front of the hood. The top and underside taper gently toward the front. Now you can see the sleek lines of the automobile.

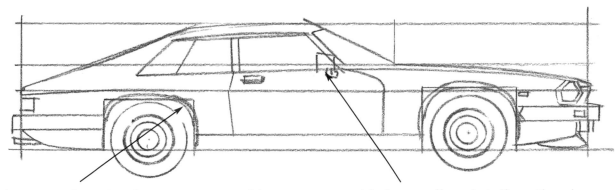

Draw in the wheel arches, which flare out slightly from the body.

Now you can add the smaller details – the door handle, wing mirror, and head- and tail-lights. Note the unusual shape of the headlights.

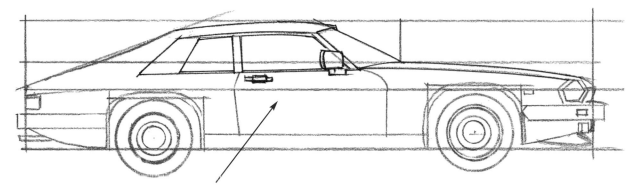

This is a luxury car, with a smooth, powerful engine and electronic seats. It is just as finely finished inside, with hand-sewn leather seats.

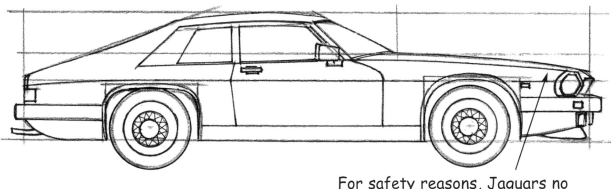

The powerful engine means this car can reach a speed of 100mph in just 16 seconds.

For safety reasons, Jaguars no longer bear the famous 'big cat' mascot on the hood, which might cause injuries in an accident.

American Truck

Huge articulated trucks travel America's freeways. These 'big rigs' are part of the American legend, and, along with their drivers, are the heroes of many road movies.

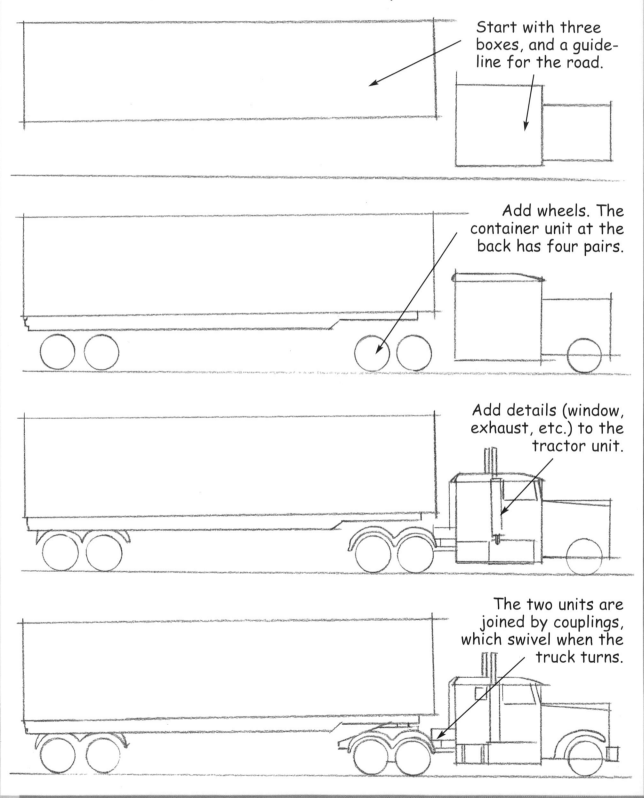

Start with three boxes, and a guide-line for the road.

Add wheels. The container unit at the back has four pairs.

Add details (window, exhaust, etc.) to the tractor unit.

The two units are joined by couplings, which swivel when the truck turns.

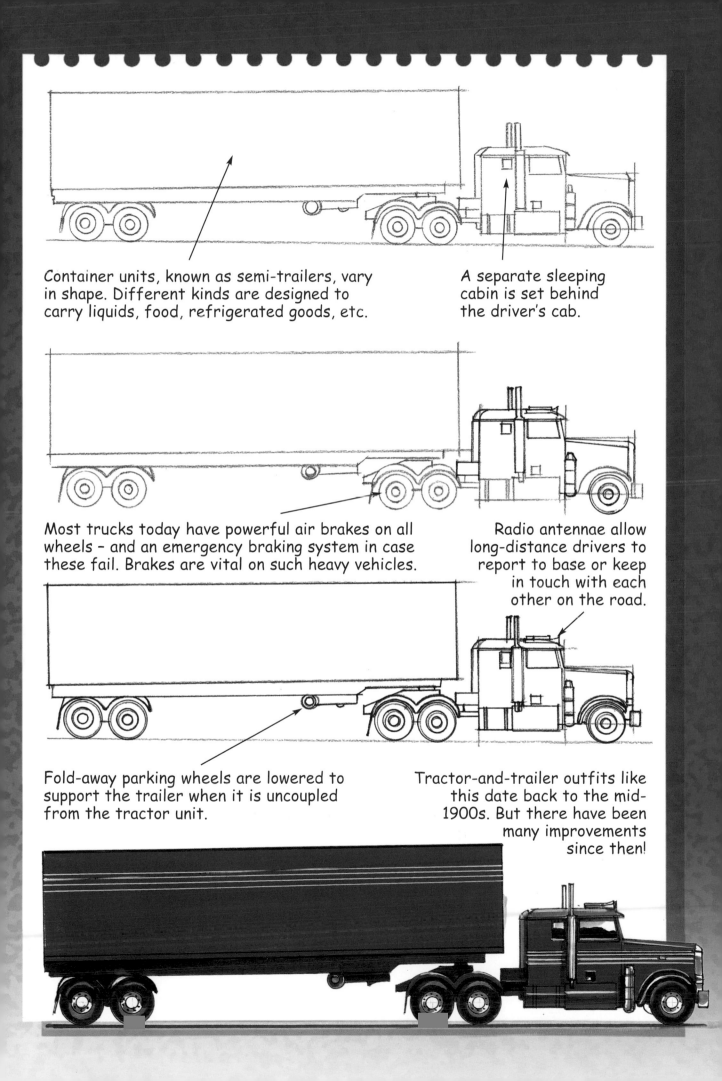

Container units, known as semi-trailers, vary in shape. Different kinds are designed to carry liquids, food, refrigerated goods, etc.

A separate sleeping cabin is set behind the driver's cab.

Most trucks today have powerful air brakes on all wheels – and an emergency braking system in case these fail. Brakes are vital on such heavy vehicles.

Radio antennae allow long-distance drivers to report to base or keep in touch with each other on the road.

Fold-away parking wheels are lowered to support the trailer when it is uncoupled from the tractor unit.

Tractor-and-trailer outfits like this date back to the mid-1900s. But there have been many improvements since then!

Dump Truck

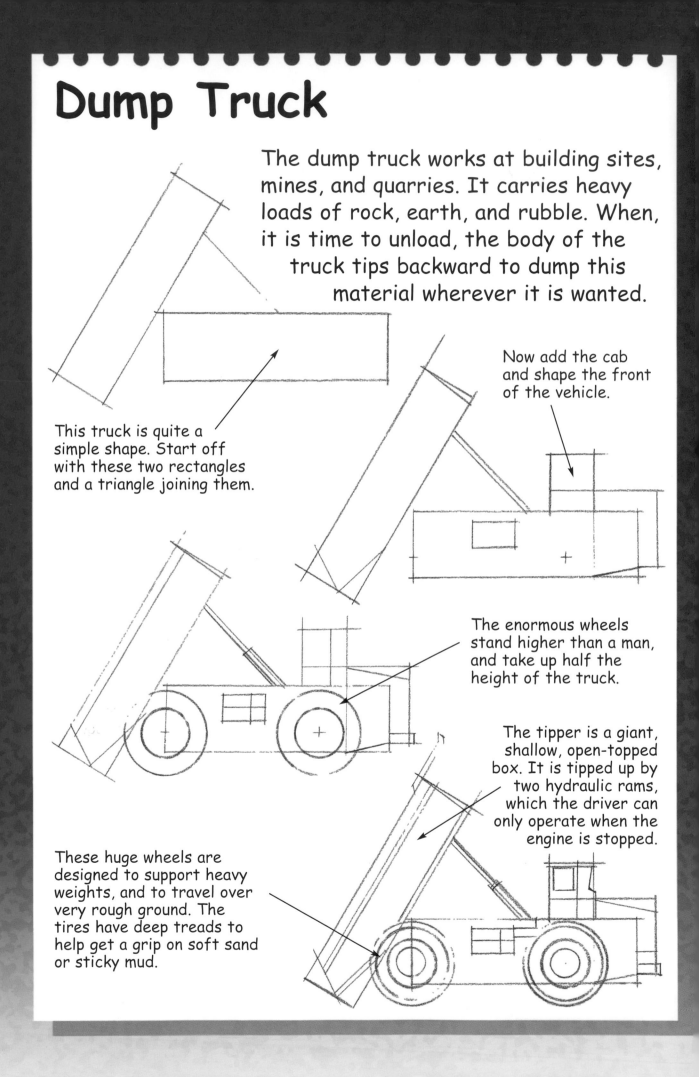

The dump truck works at building sites, mines, and quarries. It carries heavy loads of rock, earth, and rubble. When, it is time to unload, the body of the truck tips backward to dump this material wherever it is wanted.

This truck is quite a simple shape. Start off with these two rectangles and a triangle joining them.

Now add the cab and shape the front of the vehicle.

The enormous wheels stand higher than a man, and take up half the height of the truck.

The tipper is a giant, shallow, open-topped box. It is tipped up by two hydraulic rams, which the driver can only operate when the engine is stopped.

These huge wheels are designed to support heavy weights, and to travel over very rough ground. The tires have deep treads to help get a grip on soft sand or sticky mud.

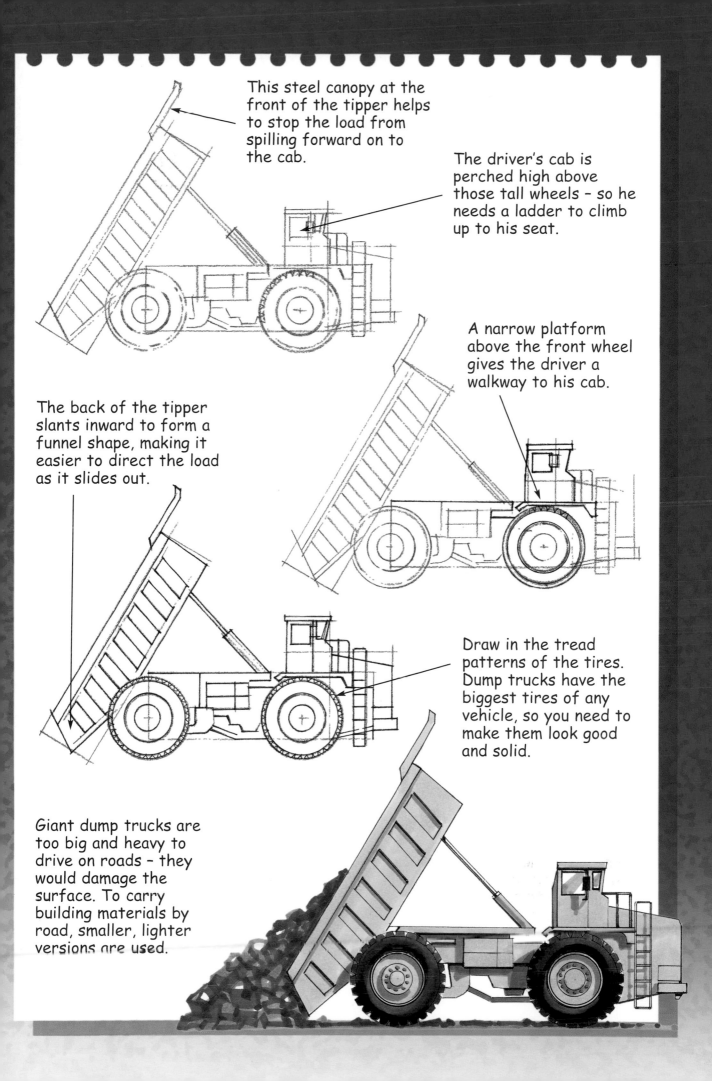

This steel canopy at the front of the tipper helps to stop the load from spilling forward on to the cab.

The driver's cab is perched high above those tall wheels – so he needs a ladder to climb up to his seat.

A narrow platform above the front wheel gives the driver a walkway to his cab.

The back of the tipper slants inward to form a funnel shape, making it easier to direct the load as it slides out.

Draw in the tread patterns of the tires. Dump trucks have the biggest tires of any vehicle, so you need to make them look good and solid.

Giant dump trucks are too big and heavy to drive on roads – they would damage the surface. To carry building materials by road, smaller, lighter versions are used.